Buddhist art and writing

Glossary

BODHI TREE When the Buddha became enlightened, he was sitting under a type of fig tree. This type of tree is sometimes called a Bodhi tree.

BODHISATTVA A being who has almost become enlightened but has chosen to stay on earth and help others to become enlightened. Bodhisattvas can be thought of as a type of saint.

THE BUDDHA The founder of Buddhism. The word Buddha means "enlightened one". The Buddha began life as a prince called Siddhartha Gautama, but he decided to leave his wealthy life and search for enlightenment. After many years of searching, he found enlightenment and taught what he had found to others.

BUDDHISM The religion that is consisting of things the Buddha taught after he found enlightenment.

ENLIGHTENMENT To be free from suffering and unhappiness. Buddhists try to reach enlightenment by meditating, studying what the Buddha taught and by doing good deeds.

FASTING Not eating for a length of time. The Buddha fasted for a long time during his search for enlightenment.

MEDITATION A way to train the mind and the body. There are many different ways to meditate, but the most common are to concentrate on a sound, an object, a picture or on your own breathing. Meditation can help anyone to concentrate better, but Buddhists believe that meditation can free you from suffering.

MONK/NUN In Buddhism, a monk/nun is a person who has decided to dedicate their lives to becoming enlightened and helping others. Some Buddhists become monks/nuns for only a short time. Buddhist monks/nuns do not marry and they own only a few possessions.

MUDRA A hand gesture. Mudras are symbols, they stand for different things, such as teaching, or wisdom. Buddhists use mudras to help a person to meditate.

NIRVANA When a person becomes enlightened, they are said to have reached nirvana. Nirvana means a person does not have any suffering in their life.

NOBLE EIGHTFOLD PATH The Buddha taught that one of the ways to end suffering and become enlightened is to follow the eightfold path. The eightfold path is a set of eight simple instructions.

SANSKRIT A form of writing used in ancient India. Many sacred Buddhist writings are written in Sanskrit.

SHRINE A place of worship. Shrines may be large or small, and they are often built at places where an important event happened. There are shrines in most religions.

SYMBOL An object, image, picture or letter that has a special meaning. Some symbols can have more than one meaning.

STUPA A type of Buddhist shrine. The first stupas were built to hold the ashes of the Buddha, but most stupas contain statues of the Buddha or ashes of Buddhist monks or other important Buddhists. Each part of the stupa has a meaning in Buddhism.

THANGKA A type of Tibetan painting that teaches a lesson about Buddhism. Thangkas are usually painted on cloth so they can be rolled up and carried.

WHEEL OF LIFE Also called the Dhammachakra wheel or the wheel of law. This is a symbol that reminds Buddhists of the first sermon the Buddha gave, where he described life as an endless wheel. Dhamma means life and chakra means wheel, and also energy.

Contents

As you go through the book, look for words in **BOLD CAPITALS**. These words are defined in the glossary.

 Understanding others

Remember that other people's beliefs are important to them. You must always be considerate and understanding when studying about faith.

Buddhist practice through art

Arts help Buddhists to understand their faith and support their meditation.

People show their faith in many ways, for example, through prayer. But there are many other ways that people can express their faith.

Art is anything that people create in order to express ideas, thoughts or feelings. Many people show their faith through arts such as painting, sculpture, writing or music. These arts can remind us of important things and teach us stories and ideas. Many religions also use symbols to help teach important ideas.

Buddhists use many types of art to show their faith. Sculptures of the Buddha and of other important Teachers, called Masters, help remind Buddhists of different parts of the Buddha's life and of his teachings.

Buddhist art can also help people to meditate. People may look at a picture or statue and meditate on its meaning. Making art is also a way for some Buddhists to earn 'merit', by creating religious objects, which helps them or others to become enlightened through meditation.

Different types of paintings are also used to help Buddhists understand the Buddha's teachings and ideals.

As Buddhism spread across the world, different styles of art and architecture were developed that reflected the styles found in different countries and regions. You can see this in the great variety of symbols and architectural features to remind Buddhists of the teachings of Buddhism.

As you read through this book, you will have a chance to explore many of the different ways that Buddhists use the arts in the practice of their faith.

◄▲ A painting showing the Buddha on his deathbed. (Inset) A Buddhist painting of a wise man meditating in a deer park as a reminder of the Buddha.

Symbols in Buddhist art

Buddhist art uses a huge number of symbols to add meaning and to remind Buddhists of the Buddha's teachings.

▶ A lotus bud used in meditation.

In the earliest centuries of Buddhism, statues of the Buddha were not used. Instead, Buddhist art consisted of images that stood for the Buddha and his teachings, such as the lotus, the Wheel of the Law, the Bodhi tree, lions and the Buddha's footprints.

As Buddhism spread, other symbols began to be used in art, such as the Tibetan Eight Auspicious Symbols and the Wheel of Life. Today, all of these symbols, and many more, are used to add meaning to Buddhist arts.

The lotus

The lotus flower was one of the first symbols to be used in Buddhist art to stand for purity.

Lotus flowers are found in ponds. The roots grow in mud, the stem grows up through the water, and the beautiful flower rests above the water, in the sunlight.

▲ A lotus in full flower.

The way the flower grows is a reminder of how the teachings of the Buddha can help people to escape from the unhappiness, or mud, of everyday life and grow into the light of enlightenment.

In art, the Buddha is often shown sitting on a lotus flower.

Other symbols

Many other symbols are used in Buddhist art. Some of these are reminders of the Buddha or of his sermons. For example, a deer may be a reminder of the Buddha's first sermon, which was given in a deer park.

Or, a picture of a Bodhi tree may be a reminder of the Buddha's enlightenment, because the Buddha became enlightened while sitting under a Bodhi tree.

A bell and a thunderbolt shape, made of metal and called a varja, are used in many Buddhist ceremonies to stand for compassion and wisdom.

▶ A lion.

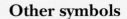

The lion is another popular symbol. Lions are thought of as being strong, powerful and 'kings' of the jungle. So, an image of a lion is often used to stand for the Buddha, who was a royal prince. The Buddha's teachings are sometimes called the 'Lion's Roar'. In Buddhist art, lions are sometimes shown carrying the throne the Buddha sits on.

The Wheel of Life

The Wheel of Life, or Dhammachakra Wheel, is a reminder of the first sermon that the Buddha gave, when he described life as an endless cycle of birth and rebirth. The wheel is usually painted or drawn with eight spokes, which stand for the Noble Eightfold Path – the path to enlightenment.

◀ Deer and a Wheel of Life decorating a Buddhist temple.

The Buddha's footprint

According to Buddhist legend, after the Buddha attained enlightenment, his feet made an imprint in the stone where he stepped.

So, drawings or carvings of the Buddha's footprints stand for the way the Buddha and his teachings are always with us. At the same time, the footprints are a reminder that the Buddha has become enlightened and is no longer on Earth, leaving just his footprints behind.

The footprints are usually made with the toes of all one length and with the symbol for the Wheel of Life (the Dhammachakra Wheel) in the centre.

The right-coiled white conch

A white conch shell stands for the beautiful sound of the teachings of the Buddha.

Golden fish

Just as a fish swims easily through the water, this symbol is a reminder that Buddhism can help people to move more easily through life, without drowning in the ocean of suffering.

Victory banner

The victory banner is a reminder that Buddhism teaches people how to win 'victory' over obstacles and suffering. It also stands for the complete victory of the mind over all harmful obstacles and negativity.

Eight Auspicious Symbols

On many Buddhist works of art, you can see eight symbols, called the Eight Auspicious Symbols. The word auspicious means 'good luck' and these symbols are each reminders of important teachings of the Buddha. These are most often used in the Tibetan Buddhist traditions.

Vase of treasure

The treasure vase stands for the wealth, happiness and long life that comes with enlightenment.

The Wheel of Life

Endless knot

This stands for the way that a person cannot become enlightened without having both wisdom and compassion.

Lotus flower

The lotus flower is a reminder of the Buddha and stands for the way that the Buddhist ideals of pure actions, pure speech and pure thoughts will help a person to leave the suffering of the world.

Precious umbrella

Just like an umbrella can protect people from sun and rain, the precious umbrella stands for the way that Buddhism can protect people from illness, harmful forces, suffering and obstacles in life.

▲ Prayer flags in blue, white, red, green and yellow.

The purpose of colour

The colours used in Buddhist art have special meanings.

Some Buddhists believe that, as the Buddha sat beneath the Bodhi tree after his enlightenment, five rays of light came out from his body and spread for miles around. The light rays were coloured yellow, blue, white, red and orange. So, in some Buddhist art these five colours are used as reminders of the Buddha's enlightenment.

Other Buddhists believe that the five most important colours are white, yellow, red, blue and green.

Using colour in meditation

Some Buddhists teach that by meditating while looking at a particular colour, a person can learn more about Buddhism and become closer to enlightenment.

For example, some Buddhists meditate while looking at the colour white, focusing on changing ignorance into wisdom; or green to change jealousy into accomplishment; or by looking at blue to help focus on changing anger into calmness.

Colour in stories

Colour is also important in many stories told about the Buddha. For example, the colour white appears in many stories told about the birth of the Buddha. Legend says that Queen Maya, the mother of the Buddha, dreamt of a white elephant that flew through the air and touched her right side with its trunk.

▼ A Buddhist temple in California, USA, decorated in the most important colours to Buddhists.

In India, where the Buddha was born, elephants are thought of as being strong and intelligent and are also reminders of rain clouds and fertility. The colour white stands for purity.

In this story, the white elephant in the dream was the unborn Buddha, who chose to be born to Queen Maya.

▲ A white elephant represents the unborn Buddha.

11

▼▶A Tibetan Buddhist painting that has many of the colours that are important to Buddhists.

Red

In Buddhism, red may stand for life and for the ability of Buddhism to change anger and other harmful thoughts into good thoughts. In Tibetan Buddhist culture, red brings good luck and protection. Monks' robes are often red.

A red lotus flower stands for the heart, love and compassion.

Blue

Blue can stand for many things, including eternity, truth, devotion, faith, purity, chastity, peace and spiritual and intellectual thought. A blue lotus flower stands for the wisdom of knowledge.

In some Buddhist traditions, turquoise jewellery is worn as a reminder of the sea and the sky. In works of art, a blue coloured Buddha is called the Buddha of Medicine or the Buddha of Healing.

Gold

Another important colour in Buddhism is gold. Statues of the Buddha are often covered with gold, or painted gold.

Gold is precious and so it is a reminder that the Buddha is precious.

White

White can stand for purity, holiness, cleanliness and honesty. It is a reminder of both life and death. The white lotus stands for enlightenment and perfection.

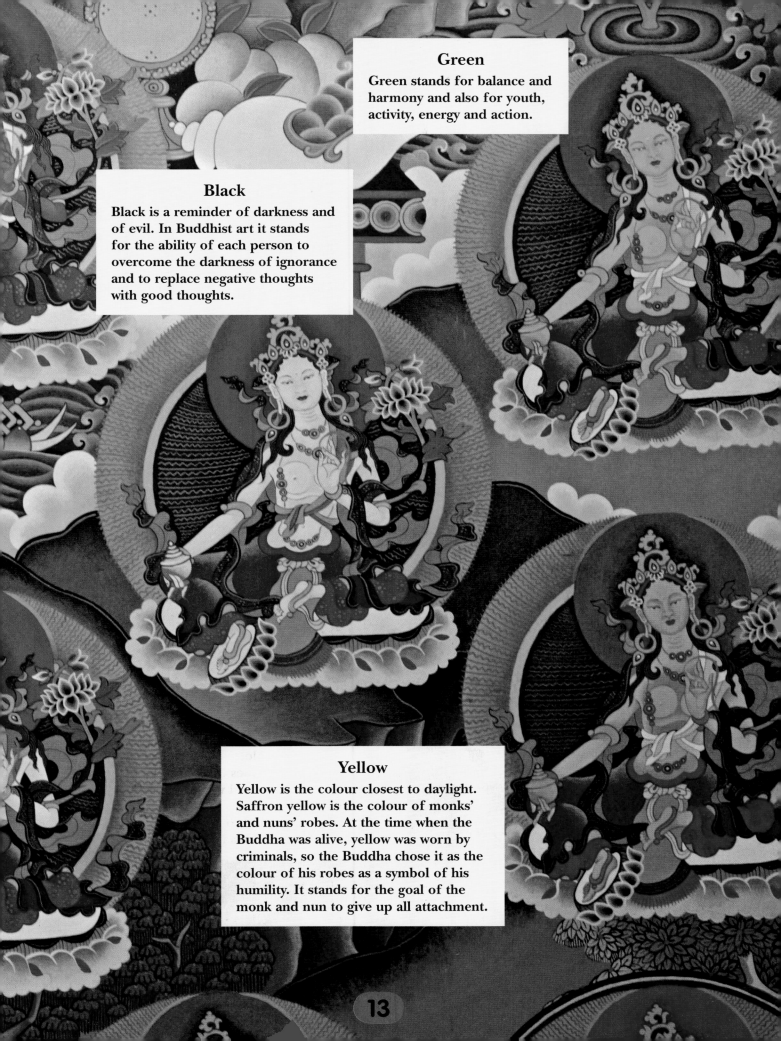

Green

Green stands for balance and harmony and also for youth, activity, energy and action.

Black

Black is a reminder of darkness and of evil. In Buddhist art it stands for the ability of each person to overcome the darkness of ignorance and to replace negative thoughts with good thoughts.

Yellow

Yellow is the colour closest to daylight. Saffron yellow is the colour of monks' and nuns' robes. At the time when the Buddha was alive, yellow was worn by criminals, so the Buddha chose it as the colour of his robes as a symbol of his humility. It stands for the goal of the monk and nun to give up all attachment.

Statues of the Buddha

Statues of the Buddha are some of the most important types of Buddhist works of art.

What statues are used for

Buddhists do not worship the statues, but they are important reminders of the Buddha and of his teachings.

Statues of the Buddha are found in almost all temples, shrines and monasteries. Some monasteries may contain hundreds of statues of all sizes, while a small shrine may contain only one statue. Many Buddhists also have statues in their homes.

Wherever they are found, the statues are used as a way to aid concentration of the mind and develop appreciation of the teachings of the Buddha.

Thinking about the features of the statue and the pose it is in helps Buddhists to focus on different teachings of the Buddha. Leaving offerings of prayers, flowers, fruit, incense, light (candles) and water in front of the statues are other ways to focus on and thank the Buddha for his teachings by practising generosity.

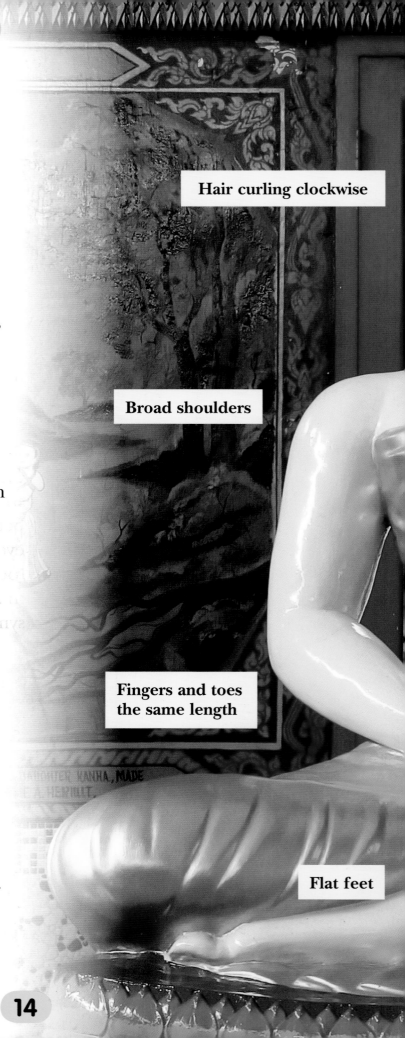

Hair curling clockwise

Broad shoulders

Fingers and toes the same length

Flat feet

▶ This statue of the Buddha shows many features that the Buddha was said to have.

Wisdom mound

Third eye

Long ear lobes

Special features

If you look at statues of the Buddha, you may notice that the Buddha always looks peaceful and calm. You may also notice that the statues all have some features in common. Each of these features has a special meaning.

Long before the Buddha was born, Indian wise men said that there were 32 marks, or features, that would be found on a great teacher. The Buddha had all of these, and some of them are usually shown on every statue of him.

Some of these special features are: a wisdom mound on the top of the head, long ear lobes (a reminder that he was a prince – his ears were stretched by wearing earrings), a spot between the eyes (also called the third eye), broad shoulders, all fingers and toes of the same length, hair curling in a clockwise direction, flat feet and symbols on the soles of his feet.

Symbols on soles of feet

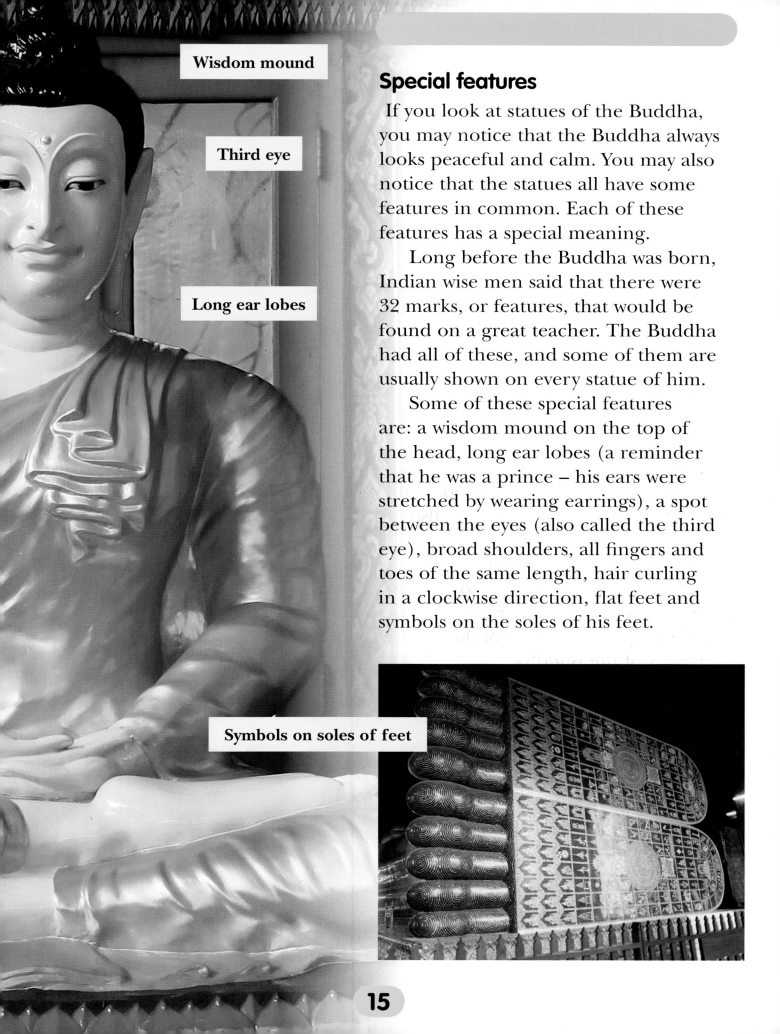

The lying or reclining position is a reminder of the Buddha's death, when he lay on his side.

Another position shows a very thin Buddha sitting in meditation. This is a reminder of a time when the Buddha tried to become enlightened by fasting (not eating). He eventually realised that this was not the right way to become enlightened.

The standing and walking Buddha may have the right foot in front. This is one of the marks of the Buddha.

Positions

Statues of the Buddha are usually found in certain positions. These change from tradition to tradition, but the most common are: sitting with legs crossed in meditation, standing, walking and lying on one side.

The sitting position is a reminder of the importance of meditation and of the moment that the Buddha became enlightened while sitting under the Bodhi tree.

Hand positions

Hand gestures, called mudras, were used by wise men in ancient India to convey special meanings. For example, a hand resting gently in the lap was a sign that we must find peace within ourselves. Most statues of the Buddha also show him using hand gestures. Buddhists can look at these hand gestures and be reminded of his teachings.

On these pages you can see some of the most common mudras and their meanings.

Vitarka mudra

This position stands for teaching and discussion. The circle formed by the thumb and index finger is the sign of the Wheel of Law. The gesture of the right hand stands for turning the Wheel of Law, while the left hand (in the dhyana mudra position) stands for meditation.

Dhammachakra mudra

This is the gesture of teaching. It is a reminder of the Buddha's first sermon, when he taught about the Wheel of Dhamma, or Wheel of Law. This gesture is sometimes called 'turning the Wheel of Law'.

The thumb and first fingers of each hand make a circle. The three remaining fingers of each hand are stretched out. The outstretched fingers of the right hand represent the people who listen to the teachings. The extended fingers of the left hand stand for the Three Jems of Buddhism – the Buddha, the Buddha's teachings and the worldwide community of Buddhists.

The hands are held in front of the heart, which shows that these teachings come straight from the Buddha's heart.

Abhaya mudra

This gesture shows an open hand, facing outwards. It is often used with a standing or walking Buddha. It is a gesture of reassurance, blessing and protection. It is also a reminder of a time when the Buddha stopped a rampaging elephant by simply raising his hand.

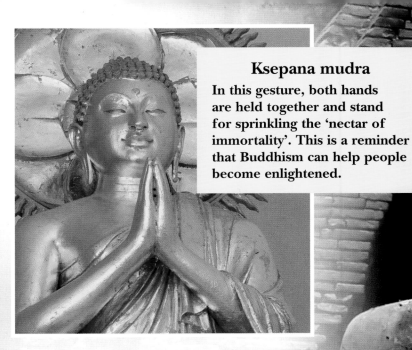

Ksepana mudra

In this gesture, both hands are held together and stand for sprinkling the 'nectar of immortality'. This is a reminder that Buddhism can help people become enlightened.

Uttarabodhi mudra

This gesture stands for enlightenment. Both hands are placed together above the head with the index fingers together and the other fingers intertwined.

Varada mudra

The hand is open but facing down. This mudra stands for the fulfilment of all wishes and is a gesture of charity.

Bhumisparsa mudra

Bhumisparsa means 'touching the earth' and this position is also called the 'earth-witness' mudra. It is a reminder of the time when the Buddha was meditating under the Bodhi tree and he was tempted by evil. He touched the ground and asked the earth to witness that he would not be tempted.

Karana mudra

This is a traditional gesture for sending away demons or bad thoughts.

Dhyana mudra

This hand gesture stands for balance and meditation. It can be made with one or both hands. When made with a single hand, the left one is placed in the lap, symbolising wisdom. An alms bowl, symbolising renunciation, may be placed in the open palm. When made with both hands, the right hand is placed above the left, with the palms facing upwards, and the fingers extended.

Sacred paintings

Different types of Buddhist paintings are used to teach important lessons about the Buddha's teachings.

Thangkas

One of the most common types of Buddhist painting is painted or embroidered on cloth scrolls or banners and is called a thangka. So, thangkas are paintings that could be rolled up and carried around, and then unrolled.

Thangkas often tell the stories of Buddhist saints and holy teachers, for example, the story of the Buddha's life. In ancient times, Buddhist teachers would use these scrolls like books, to help teach about Buddhism. Today, people look at the scrolls and think about the life of the Buddha or Buddhist Masters and teachers.

The main character of the thangka is usually painted in the centre of the scroll, and is surrounded by other characters that tell a story.

When they paint a thangka, artists do not just paint whatever they want. Instead, they usually follow certain rules. For example, they first draw a geometric grid onto the cloth and then paint everything into the squares on the grid, with the most important part in the middle. They also usually use only a few colours – black, red, yellow, blue and green are the most important.

The Wheel of Life

One of the most common subjects for thangkas is the Wheel of Life, which illustrates the cycle of reincarnation or rebirth that a person goes through before they become enlightened.

The pictures in the wheel are very scary – they are meant to show people how frightening it can be to have to repeat the cycle forever, and encourage people to escape the cycle by following the Buddha's teachings.

The main part of the wheel shows six types of life into which one can be reborn: gods, humans, animals, warlike demons, hungry spirits and hell. Each type is closer to Nirvana than the one below it. If you do good and follow the Buddha's teachings, you will be reborn into a higher type, eventually reaching Nirvana.

Mandalas

A mandala is a design that stands for Buddhist ideas and teachings. The word mandala means circle, and the mandala is usually in the shape of a circle, or a circle inside a square.

Mandalas may be paintings or drawings, and some mandalas are made from coloured sand. But a mandala is more than a pretty picture; each mandala stands for an idea, such as peace, enlightenment or the teaching of the Buddha. A mandala can also stand for the whole world, or the universe. In fact, a mandala can stand for anything that is important to the person who makes it.

Mandalas are often geometric designs, but they may include pictures of Buddhas, animals or objects.

A design used for meditation

Buddhists use the mandalas to help their meditation. Making a mandala can help a person to think about the things that are important to them, such as family and friends, or helping the environment. Some people feel that making a mandala helps them to concentrate on what is important to them.

Buddhists may look at the mandalas and meditate, or think about the meaning of the mandala. Buddhists believe that looking at a mandala can help people to feel more peaceful and happier. Making a mandala can also be a type of meditation, as we will see.

▼ A Buddhist monk making a sand mandala. The metal tool is used to place very small amounts of sand on the mandala. When it is finished, after several days, it will be brushed away.

Sand mandalas

Tibetan Buddhist monks have a tradition of making mandalas out of coloured sand. The sand is poured very slowly from small cones. It can take the monks many days or even weeks to complete a sand mandala. While they make it, the monks meditate and think about the meaning of the mandala.

Sand mandalas may also be dedicated to a particular idea. For example, they may be made in order to bring a feeling of peace to the world.

After the mandala is completed, there will be a ceremony and then the monks will destroy the mandala by brushing away the sand and pouring it into a lake or stream. This is a reminder that nothing lasts forever.

Paintings of Buddhas

When Buddhists talk about 'the Buddha' they are talking about Siddhartha Gautama, the founder of Buddhism. The Buddha was the person who taught others how to become enlightened. But Buddhists believe that there have actually been many Buddhas, or enlightened beings, throughout time. Bodhisattvas are beings who are almost enlightened and who help others to become enlightened. Buddhas and bodhisattvas are found on many Buddhist paintings and works of art.

Aksobhya
The word Aksobhya means 'immoveable' and Aksobhya is a Buddha who vowed never to be angry. He is usually shown with an angry expression and a blue complexion, holding a diamond, which stands for compassion, in one hand and touching the earth with the other.

Amida
The Amida Buddha is also called the Pure Land Buddha. He is very popular in Japanese Buddhism. One story of the Amida Buddha is that, in a previous life as a monk called Dharmakara, he vowed that he would create a land which would help people become enlightened. Anyone born in this 'pure land' would only have to be reborn one more time before becoming enlightened. In order to be born in the Pure Land the believer must have a sincere wish to be reborn there and must call upon the name of the Amida Buddha ten times.

Bhaisajyaguru
This is 'the Healing Buddha' or 'Medicine Buddha' and is said to be able to give people who call on him healing, long life, wealth and protection. His skin is either gold or blue and in one hand he holds a medicine bowl.

Maitreya

Maitreya is the future Buddha. 'Maitreya' means 'the loving one'. He is thought to bring good luck, friendliness and prosperity. In China, he is shown in statues and paintings as a fat, laughing Buddha called Hotei.

Manjusri (Manjushri)

Manjusri means 'gentle glory' and this bodhisattva brings wisdom and courage. He is often shown carrying a five-pointed sword in his right hand, which cuts through the bonds of ignorance. In his left hand, he holds a book that stands for sacred Buddhist texts.

Tara

Tara is a female bodhisattva who is said to have been formed from tears shed by another bodhisattva, who cried when he realised how many people still suffered in the world. Tara is known for her compassion and swift action to overcome fear. There are twenty-one different forms of Tara but it is Green Tara and White Tara that are the most popular.

Stupas, architecture of faith

A stupa is a type of building or shrine that has a special meaning for Buddhists.

After he died, the Buddha's body was cremated and the ashes were divided up and buried under eight burial mounds, called stupas.

In the third century BCE, after his conversion to Buddhism, the emperor Ashoka, who ruled a large part of Southeast Asia, built thousands of stupas across his empire. Some of these stupas contained the original ashes from the Buddha, and others were used as places of worship.

As Buddhism spread to new places, many more stupas were built and the shape and name of the stupa changed. Some stupas contain the ashes of Buddhist monks and holy men, others contain statues of the Buddha, and still others are simply places where people can go and think about Buddhism and the Buddha's teachings.

Shape of the stupa

The traditional shape of a stupa is a square base, topped with a dome, then steps, a parasol shape, and then a sun and moon shape and a cone shape.

▼▶Buddhist temples in Yangoon, Myanmar. Myanmar is a Buddhist country.

Each part of the stupa has several meanings. The square base stands for the earth, with each side facing one of the four directions. The dome stands for water. The steps stand for the steps that a person goes through on the way to enlightenment. The parasol shape stands for wind and for compassion, and is topped by the sun and moon, which stand for love and wisdom, and by a cone which stands for fire, or enlightenment.

The parts of the stupa may also stand for the Buddha's body, his speech and his mind, and every part of the path to enlightenment.

Stupas are also found in many other shapes. In some places they are simple square 'houses' that are often found as roadside shrines. In China, Korea and Japan, stupas are sometimes called pagodas and are shaped like tall towers with many levels. This shape stands for the journey to enlightenment, which has many parts.

▲ Buddhist stupa at the top of Benalmadena, in Spain. The tall stupa is a reminder of enlightenment and the pure mind of the Buddha.

Names for stupas in different countries	
Chaitya	Nepal
Candi	Indonesia
Chedi	Thailand
Chorten	Tibet and Bhutan
Dagoba/Chaitiya	Sri Lanka
Chedey	Cambodia
Tap	Korea
That	Laos
Ta/Pagoda	China
Tô	Japan

Stories that show faith

Stories are an important teaching tool in Buddhism.

Writing and stories are one way that Buddhist monks and teachers help people to understand the teachings of the Buddha. Many sacred writings are written in Sanskrit or other languages that are difficult for many people to read. These writings may also be difficult to understand unless a person has studied Buddhism for a long time.

But a lot of Buddhist stories are written more simply, and in plain language, so that everyone can understand the lessons of the Buddha. Some of these stories are about the life of the Buddha, and others are about ordinary people, or even animals.

In some Buddhist stories, the meaning is not obvious. People are meant to think about the story and discover for themselves what it means. This is one way of teaching Buddhist ideals.

◀ A painting showing the Buddha's first sermon to five of his followers, at the Deer Park in Sarnath. The Buddha is shown sitting on a lotus flower.

The thief and the Zen master

One evening, Zen master Shichiri Kojun was reciting holy texts when a thief entered his house with a sharp sword, demanding your "money or your life". Without any fear, Shichiri said, "Don't disturb me! Help yourself to the money, it's in that drawer". And he resumed his recitation.

The thief was startled by this unexpected reaction, but he proceeded with his business anyway. While he was helping himself to the money, the master stopped and called, "Don't take all of it. Leave some for me to pay my taxes tomorrow". The thief left some money behind and prepared to leave. Just before he left, the master suddenly shouted at him, "You took my money and you didn't even thank me?! That's not polite!". This time, the thief was really shocked at such fearlessness. He thanked the master and ran away.

The thief later told his friends that he had never been so frightened in his life.

A few days later, the thief was caught and confessed, among many others, his theft at Shichiri's house. When the master was called as a witness, he said, "No, this man did not steal anything from me. I gave him the money. He even thanked me for it."

The thief was so touched that he repented what he had done. Upon his release from prison, he became a disciple of the master and many years later, he attained enlightenment.

The four blind men and the elephant

Several people were having an argument about God, and they could not agree what God looked like. So they came to the Lord Buddha to find an answer.

The Buddha asked his disciples to get a large magnificent elephant and four blind men. He then brought the four blind men to the elephant and told them to describe it.

The first blind man touched the elephant's leg and said it was a pillar. The second blind man touched the elephant's side and said that the elephant was a wall. The third blind man touched the elephant's ear and said that it was a piece of cloth. The fourth blind man held on to the tail and described the elephant as a piece of rope. The Buddha asked the citizens: "Each blind man had touched the elephant but each of them gives a different description of the animal. Which answer is right?"

"All of them are right," was the reply.

"Why? Because everyone can only see part of the elephant. They are not able to see the whole animal. The same applies to God and to religions. No one will see Him completely." By this parable, the Lord Buddha teaches that we should respect all other legitimate religions and their beliefs.

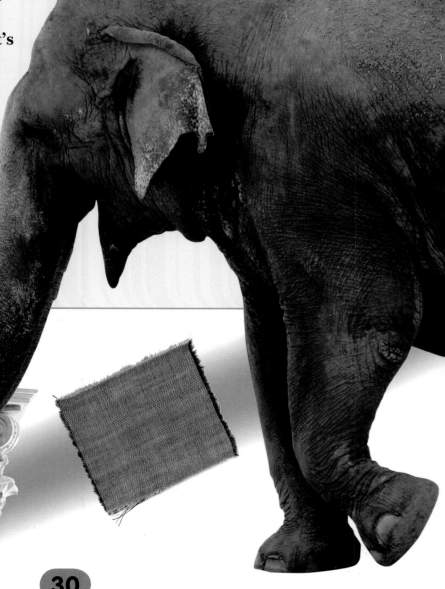

Carrying a girl across a river

One day, a Buddhist monk named I-hsiu (literally, 'One Rest') took his young student to go to town to do some business. As they approached a small river, they saw a very pretty girl walking back and forth looking very concerned.

"Lady", asked I-hsiu, "you look very concerned. What is troubling you?"

"I want to cross the river to visit my dad who is very sick, but the bridge has fallen. Where is the next nearest bridge?"

"The next closest one is many miles away. But, don't worry, I will carry you across the river."

So I-hsiu carried the girl on his back across the river. Once they reached the other side, he put her down and they went on their ways separately.

Observing the whole thing, the young student was rather uneasy. He thought, "the Master taught us that women stand for temptation, yet today he carried a pretty girl on his back across a river! That does not make any sense. Didn't the Lord Buddha teach us to keep a distance from temptation?"

Over the next couple of months, the whole thing was still bothering him in his mind. Finally, the student could not stand it any longer and raised the issue with I-hsiu.

Upon hearing this, I-hsiu burst into laughter: "I put down the girl ever since I crossed the river. You must be very tired carrying her around for the last two months!"

Index

Curriculum Visions

There's much more on-line including videos

You will find multimedia resources covering six different religions, as well as history, geography, science and spelling subjects in the subscription Professional Zone at:

www.CurriculumVisions.com

A CVP Book
Copyright Earthscape © 2008

Author
Lisa Magloff, MA

Religious Adviser
Lama Zangmo, Kagyu Samye Dzong, London Tibetan Buddhist Centre.

Senior Designer
Adele Humphries, BA

Editor
Gillian Gatehouse

Acknowledgements
The publishers would like to thank the following for their help and advice:
The Buddhapadipa Temple, Wimbledon, London and Kagyu Samye Dzong, London Tibetan Buddhist Centre, Lambeth, London.

Photographs
The Earthscape Picture Library, except: (c=centre, t=top, b=bottom, l=left, r=right)
Alamy page 24t; *Osel Shen Phen Ling (www.fpmt-osel.org)* pages 24r, 25bl, 25br;

ShutterStock pages 1, 2–3, 5 (inset), 6–7, 8–9, 10–11, 14–15 (main) 16–17, 18–19, 22–23, 24l, 25 (main), 25tl, 26–27, 28, 30–31; *TopFoto* pages 4–5 (main), 20–21.

Designed and produced by
Earthscape

Printed in China by
WKT Company Ltd

Buddhist art and writing
– *Curriculum Visions*
A CIP record for this book is available from the British Library
ISBN: 978 1 86214 246 6

This product is manufactured from sustainable managed forests. For every tree cut down at least one more is planted.